If Lost, Please Return To:

_____

Monday

Today's Goals

Tuesday

Today's Goals

Wednesday

Today's Goals

Thursday

Today's Goals

Friday

Today's Goals

Saturday

Today's Goals

Sunday

Today's Goals

Notes

Bible Study

Date:

Today's Study

Scripture

Praise

Prayer

S.O.A.P.

Scripture

Observation

Application

Prayer

Reflection

What Is This Scripture Telling Me?

Why Did God Include This Scripture In The Bible?

What Do I Need To Further Study From This Verse?

Bible Study

Date:

Today's Study

Scripture

Praise

Prayer

S.O.A.P.

Scripture

Observation

Application

Prayer

Reflection

What Is This Scripture Telling Me?

Why Did God Include This Scripture In The Bible?

What Do I Need To Further Study From This Verse?

Bible Study

Date:

Today's Study

Scripture

Praise

Prayer

S.O.A.P.

Scripture

Observation

Application

Prayer

Reflection

What Is This Scripture Telling Me?

Why Did God Include This Scripture In The Bible?

What Do I Need To Further Study From This Verse?

Bible Study

Date:

Today's Study

Scripture

Praise

Prayer

S.O.A.P.

Scripture

Observation

Application

Prayer

Reflection

What Is This Scripture Telling Me?

Why Did God Include This Scripture In The Bible?

What Do I Need To Further Study From This Verse?

Bible Study

Date:

Today's Study

Scripture

Praise

Prayer

S.O.A.P.

Scripture

Observation

Application

Prayer

Reflection

What Is This Scripture Telling Me?

Why Did God Include This Scripture In The Bible?

What Do I Need To Further Study From This Verse?

Bible Study Date:

Today's Study

Scripture

Praise

Prayer

S.O.A.P.

Scripture

Observation

Application

Prayer

Reflection

What Is This Scripture Telling Me?

Why Did God Include This Scripture In The Bible?

What Do I Need To Further Study From This Verse?

Bible Study

Date:

Today's Study

Scripture

Praise

Prayer

S.O.A.P.

Scripture

Observation

Application

Prayer

Reflection

What Is This Scripture Telling Me?

Why Did God Include This Scripture In The Bible?

What Do I Need To Further Study From This Verse?

Monday

Today's Goals

Tuesday

Today's Goals

Wednesday

Today's Goals

Thursday

Today's Goals

Friday

Today's Goals

Saturday

Today's Goals

Sunday

Today's Goals

Notes

Bible Study

Date:

Today's Study

Scripture

Praise

Prayer

S.O.A.P.

Scripture

Observation

Application

Prayer

Reflection

What Is This Scripture Telling Me?

Why Did God Include This Scripture In The Bible?

What Do I Need To Further Study From This Verse?

Bible Study

Date:

Today's Study

Scripture

Praise

Prayer

S.O.A.P.

Scripture

Observation

Application

Prayer

Reflection

What Is This Scripture Telling Me?

Why Did God Include This Scripture In The Bible?

What Do I Need To Further Study From This Verse?

Bible Study

Date:

Today's Study

Scripture

Praise

Prayer

S.O.A.P.

Scripture

Observation

Application

Prayer

Reflection

What Is This Scripture Telling Me?

_____

_____

_____

_____

Why Did God Include This Scripture In The Bible?

_____

_____

_____

_____

What Do I Need To Further Study From This Verse?

_____

_____

_____

_____

Bible Study

Date:

Today's Study

Scripture

Praise

Prayer

S.O.A.P.

Scripture

Observation

Application

Prayer

Reflection

What Is This Scripture Telling Me?

Why Did God Include This Scripture In The Bible?

What Do I Need To Further Study From This Verse?

Bible Study

Date:

Today's Study

Scripture

Praise

Prayer

S.O.A.P.

Scripture

Observation

Application

Prayer

Reflection

What Is This Scripture Telling Me?

Why Did God Include This Scripture In The Bible?

What Do I Need To Further Study From This Verse?

Bible Study

Date:

Today's Study

Scripture

Praise

Prayer

S.O.A.P.

Scripture

Observation

Application

Prayer

Reflection

What Is This Scripture Telling Me?

Why Did God Include This Scripture In The Bible?

What Do I Need To Further Study From This Verse?

Bible Study

Date:

Today's Study

Scripture

Praise

Prayer

S.O.A.P.

Scripture

Observation

Application

Prayer

Reflection

What Is This Scripture Telling Me?

Why Did God Include This Scripture In The Bible?

What Do I Need To Further Study From This Verse?

Monday

Today's Goals

Tuesday

Today's Goals

Wednesday

Today's Goals

Thursday

Today's Goals

Friday

Today's Goals

Saturday

Today's Goals

Sunday

Today's Goals

Notes

Bible Study

Date:

Today's Study

Scripture

Praise

Prayer

S.O.A.P.

Scripture

Observation

Application

Prayer

Reflection

What Is This Scripture Telling Me?

Why Did God Include This Scripture In The Bible?

What Do I Need To Further Study From This Verse?

Bible Study

Date:

Today's Study

Scripture

Praise

Prayer

S.O.A.P.

Scripture

Observation

Application

Prayer

Reflection

What Is This Scripture Telling Me?

Why Did God Include This Scripture In The Bible?

What Do I Need To Further Study From This Verse?

Bible Study

Date:

Today's Study

Scripture

Praise

Prayer

S.O.A.P.

Scripture

Observation

Application

Prayer

Reflection

What Is This Scripture Telling Me?

Why Did God Include This Scripture In The Bible?

What Do I Need To Further Study From This Verse?

Bible Study

Date:

Today's Study

Scripture

Praise

Prayer

S.O.A.P.

Scripture

Observation

Application

Prayer

Reflection

What Is This Scripture Telling Me?

Why Did God Include This Scripture In The Bible?

What Do I Need To Further Study From This Verse?

Bible Study

Date:

Today's Study

Scripture

Praise

Prayer

S.O.A.P.

Scripture

Observation

Application

Prayer

Reflection

What Is This Scripture Telling Me?

Why Did God Include This Scripture In The Bible?

What Do I Need To Further Study From This Verse?

Bible Study

Date:

Today's Study

Scripture

Praise

Prayer

S.O.A.P.

Scripture

Observation

Application

Prayer

Reflection

What Is This Scripture Telling Me?

Why Did God Include This Scripture In The Bible?

What Do I Need To Further Study From This Verse?

Bible Study

Date:

Today's Study

Scripture

Praise

Prayer

S.O.A.P.

Scripture

Observation

Application

Prayer

Reflection

What Is This Scripture Telling Me?

Why Did God Include This Scripture In The Bible?

What Do I Need To Further Study From This Verse?

Monday

Today's Goals

Tuesday

Today's Goals

Wednesday

Today's Goals

Thursday

Today's Goals

Friday

Today's Goals

Saturday

Today's Goals

Sunday

Today's Goals

Notes

Bible Study Date:

Today's Study

Scripture

Praise

Prayer

S.O.A.P.

Scripture

Observation

Application

Prayer

Reflection

What Is This Scripture Telling Me?

Why Did God Include This Scripture In The Bible?

What Do I Need To Further Study From This Verse?

Bible Study

Date:

Today's Study

Scripture

Praise

Prayer

S.O.A.P.

Scripture

Observation

Application

Prayer

Reflection

What Is This Scripture Telling Me?

Why Did God Include This Scripture In The Bible?

What Do I Need To Further Study From This Verse?

Bible Study

Date:

Today's Study

Scripture

Praise

Prayer

S.O.A.P.

Scripture

Observation

Application

Prayer

Reflection

What Is This Scripture Telling Me?

Why Did God Include This Scripture In The Bible?

What Do I Need To Further Study From This Verse?

Bible Study

Date:

Today's Study

Scripture

Praise

Prayer

S.O.A.P.

Scripture

Observation

Application

Prayer

Reflection

What Is This Scripture Telling Me?

Why Did God Include This Scripture In The Bible?

What Do I Need To Further Study From This Verse?

Bible Study

Date:

Today's Study

Scripture

Praise

Prayer

S.O.A.P.

Scripture

Observation

Application

Prayer

Reflection

What Is This Scripture Telling Me?

Why Did God Include This Scripture In The Bible?

What Do I Need To Further Study From This Verse?

Bible Study

Date:

Today's Study

Scripture

Praise

Prayer

S.O.A.P.

Scripture

Observation

Application

Prayer

Reflection

What Is This Scripture Telling Me?

Why Did God Include This Scripture In The Bible?

What Do I Need To Further Study From This Verse?

Bible Study

Date:

Today's Study

Scripture

Praise

Prayer

S.O.A.P.

Scripture

Observation

Application

Prayer

Reflection

What Is This Scripture Telling Me?

Why Did God Include This Scripture In The Bible?

What Do I Need To Further Study From This Verse?

Monday

Today's Goals

Tuesday

Today's Goals

Wednesday

Today's Goals

Thursday

Today's Goals

Friday

Today's Goals

Saturday

Today's Goals

Sunday

Today's Goals

Notes

Bible Study

Date:

Today's Study

Scripture

Praise

Prayer

S.O.A.P.

Scripture

Observation

Application

Prayer

Reflection

What Is This Scripture Telling Me?

Why Did God Include This Scripture In The Bible?

What Do I Need To Further Study From This Verse?

Bible Study

Date:

Today's Study

Scripture

Praise

Prayer

S.O.A.P.

Scripture

Observation

Application

Prayer

Reflection

What Is This Scripture Telling Me?

Why Did God Include This Scripture In The Bible?

What Do I Need To Further Study From This Verse?

Bible Study

Date:

Today's Study

Scripture

Praise

Prayer

S.O.A.P.

Scripture

Observation

Application

Prayer

Reflection

What Is This Scripture Telling Me?

Why Did God Include This Scripture In The Bible?

What Do I Need To Further Study From This Verse?

Bible Study

Date:

Today's Study

Scripture

Praise

Prayer

S.O.A.P.

Scripture

Observation

Application

Prayer

Reflection

What Is This Scripture Telling Me?

Why Did God Include This Scripture In The Bible?

What Do I Need To Further Study From This Verse?

Bible Study

Date:

Today's Study

Scripture

Praise

Prayer

S.O.A.P.

Scripture

Observation

Application

Prayer

Reflection

What Is This Scripture Telling Me?

Why Did God Include This Scripture In The Bible?

What Do I Need To Further Study From This Verse?

Bible Study

Date:

Today's Study

Scripture

Praise

Prayer

S.O.A.P.

Scripture

Observation

Application

Prayer

Reflection

What Is This Scripture Telling Me?

Why Did God Include This Scripture In The Bible?

What Do I Need To Further Study From This Verse?

Bible Study

Date:

Today's Study

Scripture

Praise

Prayer

S.O.A.P.

Scripture

Observation

Application

Prayer

Reflection

What Is This Scripture Telling Me?

Why Did God Include This Scripture In The Bible?

What Do I Need To Further Study From This Verse?

Made in the USA
Columbia, SC
02 April 2025